Platypuses

Victoria Blakemore

Copyright info/picture credits

Cover, worldswildlifewonders/Shutterstock; Page 3, Klaus/flickr; Page 5, susan flashman/AdobeStock; Page 7, Simba/AdobeStock; Page 9, PixBayBlade/Pixabay; Pages 10-11, einszweifrei/Pixabay; Page 13, 169169/AdobeStock; Page 15, susan flashman/AdobeStock; Page 17, Kevin/AdobeStock; Page 19, PIXATERRA/AdobeStock; Page 21, kovgabor79/AdobeStock; Page 23; 169169/AdobeStock; Page 25, cryptidz/wikia; Page 27, wernermuellerschell/Shutterstock; Page 29, tkremmel/Pixabay; Page 31, 169169/AdobeStock; Page 33, worldswildlifewonders/Shutterstock

Table of Contents

What Are Platypuses?

Platypuses are small mammals. They are one of the only mammals that lays eggs. They are related to the echidna, which also lays eggs.

The platypus is thought to be a strange animal. It has a bill like a duck, a tail like a beaver, and webbed feet.

Platypuses are usually light or dark brown in color. They may have white spots around their eyes.

Size

On average, an adult platypus

is usually around fifteen inches

in length. Their tail adds

another five inches to their

length.

Platypuses are not very heavy.

When fully grown, they often

weigh about three pounds.

Male platypuses are usually

larger than female platypuses.

Platypuses have a large bill that looks like a duck's bill. It helps them to find food and scoop it up.

They have webbed feet. This webbing helps them to swim. When they are on land, it **retracts** so they can use their claws to dig.

6

They have special folds of skin that cover their eyes and ears. They can also completely close their nostrils. This helps them to swim and stay underwater.

Habitat

Platypuses are found in **freshwater** habitats such as lakes, ponds, rivers, and streams.

They are usually found along the water's edge. They dig a burrow into the dirt and mud near the water.

Range

Platypuses are found in parts of eastern and southern Australia.

Most are found on the mainland.

Some live on Kangaroo island, an

island off the coast of Australia.

Diet

Platypuses are **carnivores**.

They eat only meat.

Their diet is usually made

up of insects, larvae,

shellfish, and worms. They

may also eat small frogs or

fish.

A platypus bill has special

electroreceptors. They help the

platypus to sense food in the

water.

Platypuses use their bill to scoop up food and gravel from underwater. They do not have teeth, so they use the gravel to help them grind up the food on the roof of their mouth.

They do not have a stomach. They are able to digest their food completely without one.

Platypuses store about half of

their body fat in their tail. If food

is **scarce**, they may use some of

that fat to survive.

Communication

Not much is known about how

platypuses communicate with

each other.

Male platypuses have a spur on

their **hind** leg. It has a special

venom that can be used to

help the platypus defend itself

against other animals, including

other platypuses.

Platypuses have been heard

growling as a warning if they

are bothered.

Movement

Platypuses use their front limbs to paddle. Their **hind** limbs and tail are used to help them steer.

Their thick, waterproof fur helps to keep them warm and dry while they are in the water.

Platypuses are much slower

on land than they are in the

water.

Platypus Eggs

The mother lays one or two eggs at a time. She uses her tail to hold them against her body to keep them warm.

After about ten days, the eggs hatch. The young platypuses are about the size of a lima bean.

Platypuses are able to swim by themselves after three or four months.

Platypus Life

Most platypuses are **solitary**. They spend most of their time alone.

They are also **nocturnal**, which means that they are most active at night. Many spend the day resting in burrows they dig into the dirt and mud at the water's edge.

Platypuses can be very **territorial**. They do not like other platypuses coming too close to their space.

Platypus Burrows

Platypus burrows are dug into the dirt and mud at the water's edge. They usually have a long entrance tunnel.

At the end of the entrance tunnel is a **chamber** where the platypus rests during the day. Some burrows may have more than one chamber.

Burrows help platypuses to stay safe from predators. They provide them with **shelter** from the sun.

Population

Platypuses are not **endangered**, but their populations have begun to **decline** in some places.

Researchers do not know how many platypuses there are in the wild. They have to **estimate** because platypuses can be hard to find.

In the wild, platypuses can live

to be about twenty years old.

Platypuses in Danger

There are two main threats that platypuses are facing: habitat loss and pollution.

With more construction taking place, many platypus habitats are being harmed. They need **undisturbed** land around the water's edge to build burrows.

In some places, **pollution** is affecting the water quality. This can make platypuses sick.

Helping Platypuses

Many people are trying to help platypuses. There are people who go to platypus habitats and clean them up by picking up trash.

There are laws in Australia that make it **illegal** to pollute the water. These laws can help to protect platypus habitats.

In some places, construction close to the water has been limited. This prevents platypus habitats from being destroyed.

Some groups focus on education. They want to teach people about the platypus. They hope that people will want to help if they know more about platypuses.

Glossary

Carnivore: an animal that eats only meat

Chamber: a room

Decline: get smaller

Electroreceptors: special parts of an animal that allow them to sense other animals in the water

Endangered: at risk of becoming extinct

Estimate: to make a guess

Freshwater: water that does not contain salt

Hind: back

Illegal: against the law

Nocturnal: animals that are active at night

Pollution: harmful materials that can be in the air, water, and soil

Retract: pull back in

Scarce: hard to find

Shelter: a place that provides protection from the weather

Solitary: living alone

Territorial: when an animal is protective of its territory

Undisturbed: not bothered

Venom: a poison produced by some animals

About the Author

Victoria Blakemore is a first grade

teacher in Southwest Florida with a

passion for reading.

You can visit her at

www.elementaryexplorers.com

Also in This Series

Gray Wolves	Sloths	Flamingos	Camels	Koalas	Honey Bees
Pandas	Pangolins	White-Tailed Deer	Orcas	Giraffes	Corn
Meerkats	Echidnas	Walruses	Raccoons	Bald Eagles	Apples
Arctic Foxes	Red Pandas	Cassowaries	Tigers	Ladybugs	Moose
Beluga Whales	Leopards	Elephants	Jellyfish	Binturongs	Lions
Dolphins	Reindeer	Hammerhead Sharks	Hippos	Pumpkins	Peafowl

Elementary Explorers

Victoria Blakemore

Also in This Series

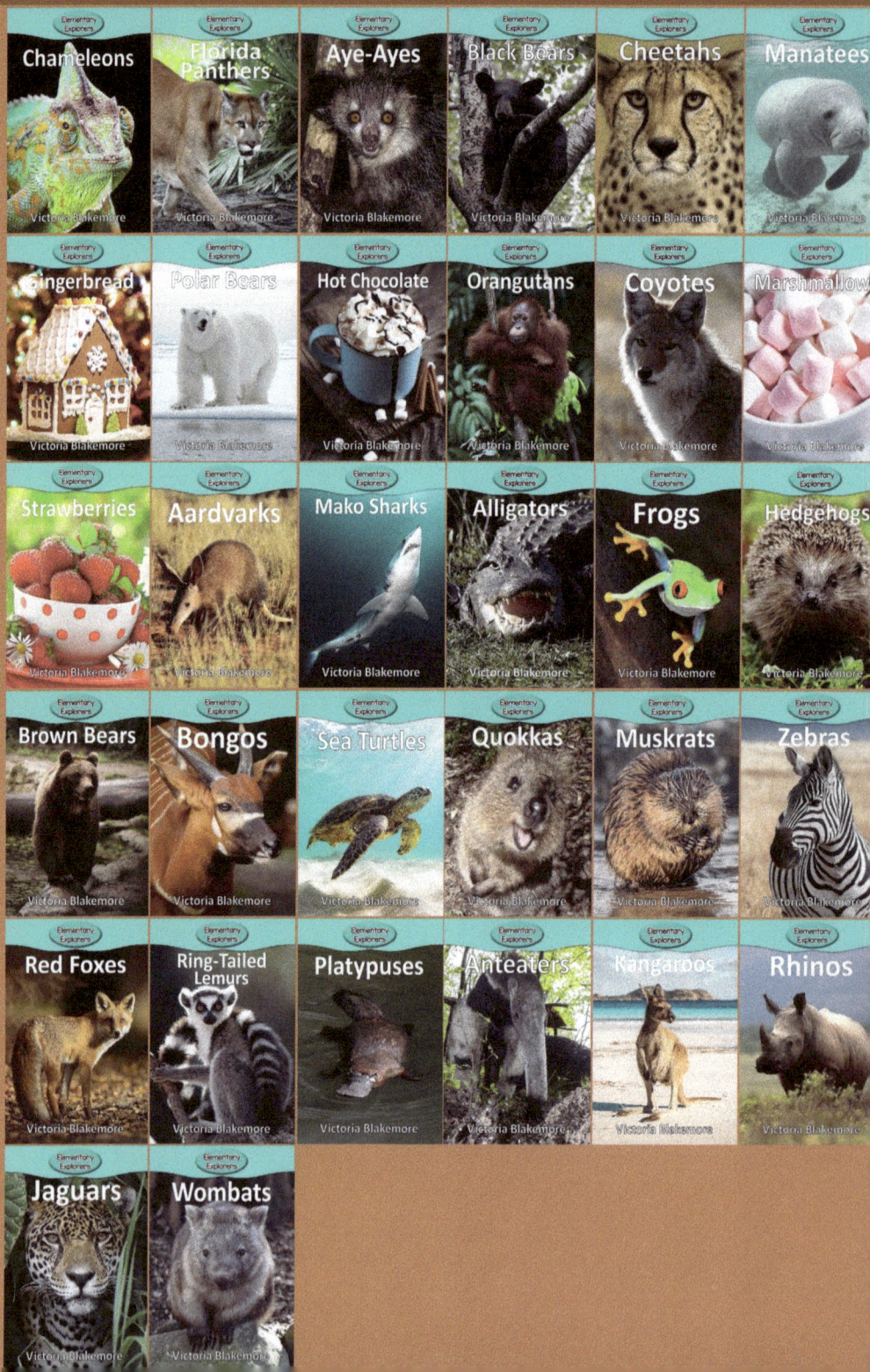

Chameleons	Florida Panthers	Aye-Ayes	Black Bears	Cheetahs	Manatees
Gingerbread	Polar Bears	Hot Chocolate	Orangutans	Coyotes	Marshmallow
Strawberries	Aardvarks	Mako Sharks	Alligators	Frogs	Hedgehogs
Brown Bears	Bongos	Sea Turtles	Quokkas	Muskrats	Zebras
Red Foxes	Ring-Tailed Lemurs	Platypuses	Anteaters	Kangaroos	Rhinos
Jaguars	Wombats				

www.ingramcontent.com/pod-product-compliance
Lightning Source LLC
Chambersburg PA
CBHW051253020426
42333CB00025B/3185